21st Century Skills Library

REAL WORLD MATH: SPORTS

RUNNING

Katie Marsico and Cecilia Minden

Cherry Lake Publishing
Ann Arbor, Michigan

Published in the United States of America by Cherry Lake Publishing
Ann Arbor, Michigan
www.cherrylakepublishing.com

Math Adviser: Tonya Walker, MA, Boston University

Content Adviser: Thomas Sawyer, EdD, Professor of Recreation and Sport Management, Indiana State University

Photo Credits: Cover and page 1, ©iStockphoto.com/Jacom Stephens; page 4, ©iStockphoto.com/Millanovic; page 6, ©Bruce Yeung, used under license from Shutterstock, Inc.; page 9, ©iStockphoto.com/Artist85; page 10, ©Shawn Pecor, used under license from Shutterstock, Inc.; page 12, ©iStockphoto.com/vandervelden; page 14, ©Galina Barskaya, used under license from Shutterstock, Inc.; page 16, ©AP Photo, page 18, ©Mauricio-José Schwarz/Alamy; page 21, ©iStockphoto.com/yenwen; page 22, ©Associated Sports Photography/Alamy; page 25, ©iStockphoto.com/vndrpttn

Library of Congress Cataloging-in-Publication Data
Marsico, Katie, 1980–
 Running / by Katie Marsico and Cecilia Minden.
    p. cm.—(Real world math)
 Includes bibliographical references and index.
 ISBN-13: 978-1-60279-249-4
 ISBN-10: 1-60279-249-6
 1. Running—Juvenile literature. 2. Track and field—Juvenile literature.
3. Arithmetic—Problems, exercises, etc.—Juvenile literature. I. Minden, Cecilia. II. Title. III. Series.
 GV1061.M37 2009
 796.42—dc22   2008001167

Cherry Lake Publishing would like to acknowledge the work of
The Partnership for 21st Century Skills.
Please visit www.21stcenturyskills.org *for more information.*

TABLE OF CONTENTS

CHAPTER ONE
Cross the Finish Line!   4

CHAPTER TWO
A Few Running Basics   9

CHAPTER THREE
Do the Math: Impressive Pros   16

CHAPTER FOUR
Do the Math: Remarkable Running Records   21

CHAPTER FIVE
Get Your Own Race Going!   25

Real World Math Challenge Answers   29

Glossary   30

For More Information   31

Index   32

About the Authors   32

CROSS THE FINISH LINE!

Competitive running is a fast-paced sport that requires training and determination.

The stands around you are filled with cheering crowds. The faces of your **competitors** seem to blur as you speed past them. You can sense that all your hard training is paying off as you complete the final stretch of the 100-meter sprint. You've worked hard to build **endurance**. But will you have enough energy to blast across the finish line ahead of everyone else?

You dash past one last runner and gallop over the finish line. You are the official champion in the 100-meter sprint! Being an amazing athlete was not the only thing that gave you a winning edge today. Would you have guessed that math skills were also important to your success on the track?

REAL WORLD MATH CHALLENGE

Sara is running in a 200-meter sprint and finishes in 40 seconds. Ella finishes in 50 seconds. **How much faster is Sara? What is the average number of meters Sara runs per second? What is the average number of meters Ella runs per second?**

(Turn to page 29 for the answers)

How is math related to running? First, you need to understand a bit about the history of running as a sport. Track races date back to ancient Greece. The first Olympic Games were in 776 BC. Centuries later, people in 19th-century England began setting rules for track competitions. Track races were part of the first modern Olympic Games in 1896. The rules that were set then are still used today.

Many track-and-field events, including the high jump, require running, timing, and math.

Running is at the center of many competitions. Certain races take place in stadiums. These are usually called track-and-field events. Track-and-field sports are referred to as athletics. Competitions are called meets.

The track wraps around an area called the infield. The infield is often where field events occur, such as throwing and jumping. Throwing events are shot put, hammer, javelin, and discus.

Jumping events include the high jump, pole

vault, long jump, and triple jump.

Some competitions involve runners leaping

over hurdles, crossing shallow pools of water

called water jumps, and clearing barriers. A

few events include a combination of running,

jumping, and throwing.

An organization named USA Track and Field

(USATF) oversees track-and-field events in the

United States. The International Association of

Athletics Federations (IAAF) oversees track-and-

field events all over the world. The IAAF is made

21st Century Content

The Olympics are truly a global event. Nearly every country on Earth is represented at the Games. Athletes representing their particular country compete side by side. It is considered a great honor to be chosen as the host country for the Olympics. As guests in the host country, athletes become exposed to new languages and even new foods. In 2008, the Summer Olympics were held in Beijing, China.

up of 212 member countries. This group sponsors a series of international track competitions called the World Cup, which occurs every four years.

Does every race have to take place on an official track? Absolutely not! Other races occur on **courses** that travel through open grassy areas, woods, and even over water. These races make up cross-country running.

Can you guess where road running takes place? On a road, of course! Trail running occurs on hiking trails. Fell running takes athletes over mountains and hills. Some runners participate in ultramarathons, which are races that cover longer distances than standard marathons.

You can see that athletes run in many different settings. We will pay the most attention to track running for the moment. Now's the perfect time to discover how math helps make first-place racers. So tie up your running shoes and reach for your calculator. Get set to sprint to the finish line!

CHAPTER TWO

A Few Running Basics

Running tracks can vary in size, color, and surface material.

It might look easy to move fast on a track. Not necessarily! There is much more to competitive running than simply moving fast. Measurements and math are a major part of track races.

Athletes can run on either an indoor or outdoor court. Outdoor tracks are usually oval shaped with a 400-meter **circumference**. These tracks are often coated with rubber or asphalt. They have six to ten lanes, though most outdoor tracks have eight.

This middle school student runs one leg of a relay race carrying a baton.

Indoor tracks are generally smaller. These tracks have four to six lanes and a circumference of about 200 meters. They are usually made from rubber or wood.

Track races vary depending on the distances being run. There are usually separate races for men and women. Outdoor track races feature 100-meter, 200-meter, and 400-meter sprints. Indoor sprints include 50-meter, 60-meter, 200-meter, and 400-meter events. Middle-distance competitions can stretch from 600 meters to 3,000 meters. Middle-distance athletes also sometimes participate in a mile run. Runners in long-distance events typically run either 5,000 meters or 10,000 meters.

Relay races are another type of track competition. Runners in these events rely on teamwork. Relay races are divided into four sections. These sections are called legs. One runner is responsible for each leg. Athletes in relays carry a baton and pass it to teammates as they complete their leg of the race. The pass must occur in an area of the track called the exchange zone. The exchange zone measures 20 meters in length.

REAL WORLD MATH CHALLENGE

Jackson and Matt each belong to track teams. Jackson has competed in three 200-meter sprints. Matt has participated in two 800-meter middle-distance races. **What is the total number of meters Jackson has run up to this point? How about Matt? Both boys hope to run 2,000 meters by the end of the track season. What percentage of this goal has each run so far?**

(Turn to page 29 for the answers)

Marathons, races of more than 26 miles (42 kilometers), usually take place on open roads.

In a 4 x 100-meter relay, four runners cover a distance of 100 meters each. In a 4 x 400-meter relay, four runners travel a distance of 400 meters each. Most relay teams have four runners. Distances can vary.

Running events in track-and-field competitions may take place on open roads instead of tracks. Sometimes racers jump over hurdles. For the moment, we will stay focused on track races that strictly feature running.

In **professional** track events, the scoring is not based on how the team does. For example, no single country is ever declared a champion in

Olympic track competitions. Instead, Olympic officials focus on the performances of individual runners. They time how long it takes them to complete a particular race.

Track races do not last a set amount of time. Some sprints take athletes several seconds. Long-distance events can last closer to 30 minutes. Races end when every athlete who is running completes the distance.

Different races require different skills, too. For example, sprinters need to move quickly over shorter stretches, instead of pacing themselves. Long-distance runners must be speedy, but they

It is important to wear comfortable running shoes that give good support and grip.

must also maintain their energy. They will be exhausted by the finish line if they simply sprint as fast as they can the entire race.

How runners dress is an important part of how well they perform. Most wear lightweight shorts and tank tops or sleeveless athletic jerseys called singlets. They pick clothes that give them speed, comfort, and flexibility and that prevent overheating. Runners on track teams may all wear specially colored uniforms. Individual athletes also pin a number on their clothes so officials and fans can identify them.

You may not be surprised to learn that runners need to wear special shoes. Track shoes have spikes on the bottom. These spikes help athletes run fast without slipping or sliding. Some shoes are built especially for sprinters. Others are designed for runners traveling greater distances.

Athletes on the track have to follow certain rules no matter how far or fast they are running. Participants in a race must always stay in their lane. They can never purposely block another runner or halt their progress. Officials decide if an athlete has broken a rule. This is called committing a foul. Certain fouls can disqualify runners from a race.

Luckily, paying close attention to numbers will get you from start to finish. Using your math skills on the track will help you move faster. It will also speed up how quickly you learn the measurements and rules of running!

CHAPTER THREE

DO THE MATH: IMPRESSIVE PROS

Can you imagine winning an Olympic gold medal? Professional runners

win fans and fame with their amazing talent on the track. Wilma Rudolph,

an athlete from Tennessee, is one unforgettable example. She was the first

American sprinter Wilma Rudolph holds flowers and medals after winning two 1961 races in Moscow, Russia.

American woman runner to claim three Olympic gold medals in a single game. And she did it all with a sprained ankle!

Rudolph wowed crowds during the Olympics in Rome in 1960. She earned the gold for the women's 100-meter and 200-meter sprints and for the women's 4 x 100-meter relay. Rudolph refused to be slowed down by the brutal heat or her ankle injury. The 100-meter race took her only 11 seconds. She broke Olympic records in the 200-meter sprint, finishing the event in 24 seconds. Rudolph and her teammates finished the relay in a stunning 44.5 seconds.

Rudolph won many honors besides her gold medals. Several sports groups declared her Athlete of the Year in 1960. Later, in 1983, she was welcomed into the U.S. Olympic Hall of Fame. Her speed and intensity earned her the nickname "Tennessee Tornado."

As a child, Wilma Rudolph became ill with polio, a disease that seriously damaged her leg. Yet her determination was strong. She was committed to learning how to walk with a leg brace, and later, with a special shoe. Eventually, she was able to walk on her own. This same determination helped Rudolph overcome cultural and gender barriers in the athletic world and become one of the greatest female African American athletes of all time.

Moroccan runner Hicham El Guerrouj stands with a group of young fans. He holds several middle-distance world records.

Track has many remarkable male runners,

too. Hicham El Guerrouj (HEE-shum ELL gah-

ROODGE) is a famous middle-distance runner from

Morocco. One of his world records came in 1999 when he ran the men's mile in 3 minutes, 43 seconds, and 13 milliseconds. He also set a world record for the men's outdoor 2,000-meter race in 1999. That event only took him 4 minutes, 44 seconds, and 79 milliseconds. No other runner has beat these world records yet.

El Guerrouj won two Olympic gold medals in Greece in 2004. This speedy athlete retired in 2006 but left some terrific career **statistics** behind him.

REAL WORLD MATH CHALLENGE

El Guerrouj set a world record by finishing a 1,500-meter race in 3 minutes and 26 seconds in 1998. **How many total seconds does his time come to?** Remember that there are 60 seconds in 1 minute. **What is the average number of meters he ran per second?**

(Turn to page 29 for the answers)

Track runners are recognized for their athletic abilities in many ways. Several win trophies and medals. Others are named players of the year or world champions. Some, such as Rudolph, even enter the Olympic Hall of Fame. There are usually different awards for men and women.

Runners' numbers can earn them fans. Their numbers also affect the numbers in their bank accounts. Track stars often win large sums of prize money. A 2003 report noted that middle-distance runner Maria Mutola from Mozambique made $1,330,624 in prize money alone. It is clear that speed on the track can lead to some spectacular digits!

REAL WORLD MATH CHALLENGE

U.S. sprinter Justin Gatlin is said to have earned about $600,000 in prize money in 2003. He won about $500,000 at a race in Russia that year. **What percentage of his total earnings did he claim in Russia? How much money did he win from other competitions?**

(Turn to page 29 for the answers)

CHAPTER FOUR

DO THE MATH: REMARKABLE RUNNING RECORDS

Setting any running record takes a lot of work!

How long do you think it would take you to run 10,000 meters? That distance is a little more than the length of 90 football fields. Ethiopian runner Kenenisa Bekele (ken-eh-NEE-sah BEK-eh-lah) did it in just 26 minutes, 17 seconds, and 53 milliseconds in 2005! He set the IAAF men's record for that distance.

Maybe you plan on beating the IAAF record for sprinting instead. You will still have to be very speedy. No one has been able to top U.S. runner

Who set the IAAF record for the boys' 100-meter sprint? Sixteen-year-old Rynell Parson finished the event in 10 seconds and 23 milliseconds in 2007.

Rynell would not be such a great athlete if he didn't use his time effectively. He is a busy teenager who has figured out how to balance school, practice, and friends. His parents help make sure that his grades don't suffer because of his sprinting.

Michael Johnson of the United States won a gold medal in the 400-meter race at the 1996 Olympic Games.

Florence Griffith Joyner's record for the women's 100-meter race. In 1988, she finished that event in 10 seconds and 49 milliseconds.

You don't have to be an adult to make history with amazing numbers.

Chandra Cheeseborough (CHAN-drah CHEEZ-bur-oh) sprinted 100

meters in 11 seconds and 13 milliseconds. She was only 17 when she set

the girls' IAAF record in that event in 1976.

REAL WORLD MATH CHALLENGE

Florence Griffith Joyner set the IAAF record for the women's 100-meter sprint
in 1988 with a time of 10.49. Her time beat Chandra Cheeseborough's girls'
100-meter IAAF record of 11.13, set in 1976. **How much faster was Griffith
Joyner's time than Cheeseborough's 1976 record time?**

(Turn to page 29 for the answer)

Some track runners are famous for making their mark in the Olympics.

U.S. star Michael Johnson won five gold medals in track races. He also set

three Olympic records. Johnson has proven himself the fastest runner in

the men's 200-meter and 400-meter races.

In fact, U.S. runners have earned several Olympic records for their country. Team USA holds leading times in two men's sprints and both men's relay events. A U.S. athlete has also set records in two women's sprints.

REAL WORLD MATH CHALLENGE

Both Johnson and Griffith Joyner have set Olympic records in 200-meter sprints. Johnson clocked in at 19 seconds and 32 milliseconds. Griffith Joyner finished in 21 seconds and 34 milliseconds. **How many total milliseconds did the races take each runner?** Remember that there are 1,000 milliseconds in a second. **How many more milliseconds did Griffith Joyner take to finish the event than Johnson?**

(Turn to page 29 for the answers)

Can you see how numbers make track runners and their home countries famous for years to come? Even a fraction of a second can change an athlete's career forever. Maybe someday you will be the one who clocks in at an unbelievable speed!

CHAPTER FIVE

GET YOUR OWN RACE GOING!

Do you have to be a trained track pro to enjoy a race? No way! Many colleges, high schools, and grade schools have track teams. Or you can arrange a race with your friends.

A school track team huddles before a track meet.

You do not have to compete against someone else to have fun on the track. Many people prefer running or jogging on their own. A lot of people run to relax and get exercise.

Many runners prefer running on a track since it is usually clean and safe. You will also probably have an easier time measuring the distances you run on a track. Your local park or a nearby school might have a track you can use. Many fitness centers have tracks, too.

You will have to choose a running outfit once you pick a track. Your choice of clothes will depend on where you are running and the weather. T-shirts, tank tops, and shorts will help you stay cool when running in outdoor heat or on an inside track. A hooded sweatshirt and sweatpants are smart choices when using an outdoor track in cooler temperatures. Be careful not to overdress though, since you want to stay cool enough to continue running.

Always wear running shoes or track shoes when you hit the track. Make sure that the bottoms of your shoes are not too worn and that your laces are tied. Do not forget to wear socks. They cushion your feet and absorb sweat as you move.

You will also need a stopwatch if you plan to keep track of times. Pack a bottle

of water, too. Water keeps people's bodies healthy and energized as they exercise.

REAL WORLD MATH CHALLENGE

Tia wants to buy track shoes. The pair she likes costs $50.00. She has already saved $10.00. **How much money does she still need? What percentage of the total cost does she have in savings?**

(Turn to page 29 for the answers)

Staying comfortable and safe is extremely important in running. So

is setting guidelines if you plan to race with friends. The biggest thing to

remember is that you should always be a good sport. Friendship and fun

should mean more to you than winning every race.

Running does not have to be done on a track. Jogging trails or even

neighborhood sidewalks will do the job. Just be sure that you are not

running close to traffic or on slippery or uneven surfaces.

21st Century Content

Runners who compete in marathons must build their endurance. The Olympic marathon covers 42.195 kilometers (26 miles and 385 yards)! Endurance is not built overnight, so don't push yourself. Being a good athlete means making your health a priority and listening to your body. Pain could mean something's wrong, so you should get help immediately. Understanding and taking certain preventive steps will help make you a better athlete. Stretch before and after physical activity, and increase the intensity of your workouts gradually.

Sometimes you may prefer to simply watch a race. Many running fans like attending marathons. These races often raise money and awareness to help people who are sick or in need. You show your support for your entire community when you cheer for marathon runners.

Do not worry if you are not quite ready to run in a marathon or on a track team. It takes practice to build speed and endurance. Math skills are always certain to bring you closer to the gold. Are you all set to hit the track? You have practiced addition, subtraction, multiplication, and division. Now be the first to cross the finish line!

REAL WORLD MATH CHALLENGE ANSWERS

Chapter One
Page 5

Sara is 10 seconds faster than Ella.

50 seconds − 40 seconds = 10 seconds

Sara runs an average of 5 meters per second.

200 meters ÷ 40 seconds = 5 meters per second

Ella runs an average of 4 meters per second.

200 meters ÷ 50 seconds = 4 meters per second

Chapter Two
Page 11

Jackson has run a total of 600 meters.

3 sprints x 200 meters = 600 meters

Matt has run a total of 1,600 meters.

2 races x 800 meters = 1,600 meters

Jackson has covered 30 percent of his running goal.

600 meters ÷ 2,000 meters = 0.30 = 30%

Matt has covered 80 percent of his running goal.

1,600 meters ÷ 2,000 meters = 0.80 = 80%

Chapter Three
Page 19

El Guerrouj took a total of 206 seconds to finish the race.

3 minutes x 60 seconds = 180 seconds

180 seconds + 26 seconds = 206 seconds

He ran an average of 7.28 meters per second.

1,500 meters ÷ 206 seconds = 7.28 meters per second

Page 20

Gatlin claimed 83 percent of his earnings in Russia.

$500,000 ÷ $600,000 = 0.83 = 83%

He won $100,000 in other competitions.

$600,000 − $500,000 = $100,000

Chapter Four
Page 23

Griffith Joyner's time was 0.64 seconds faster than Cheeseborough's record time.

11.13 seconds - 10.49 seconds = 0.64 seconds

Page 24

The race took Johnson 19,032 milliseconds.

19 seconds x 1,000 = 19,000 milliseconds

19,000 milliseconds + 32 milliseconds = 19,032 milliseconds

Griffith Joyner completed her event in 21,034 milliseconds.

21 seconds x 1,000 = 21,000 milliseconds

21,000 milliseconds + 34 milliseconds = 21,034 milliseconds

It took Griffith Joyner 2,002 more milliseconds to finish the race.

21,034 milliseconds − 19,032 milliseconds = 2,002 milliseconds

Chapter Five
Page 27

Tia still needs $40.00.

$50.00 − $10.00 = $40.00

She currently has 20 percent of the total amount saved up.

$10.00 ÷ $50.00 = 0.20 = 20%

Glossary

circumference (sir-KUM-frents) the boundary line around a circle

competitors (kuhm-PEH-tuh-turz) rivals or opponents in a race or sporting event

courses (KORS-ehz) paths used in a race or sporting event

endurance (in-DUR-uns) the ability to keep up intense exercise or activity over an extended period of time

milliseconds (MI-luh-seh-kundz) units of measurement that make up one thousandth of a second

professional (pruh-FESH-uh-nuhl) describing a sport that is played for money or as a career

statistics (steh-TISS-tiks) a branch of math that deals with the collection and interpretation of numbers and information

FOR MORE INFORMATION

Books

Belval, Brian. *Olympic Track and Field*. New York: Rosen Publishing, 2007.

Braun, Eric. *Wilma Rudolph*. Mankato, MN: Capstone Press, 2006.

Web Sites

International Association of Athletics Federations
www.iaaf.org
Find up-to-date information on upcoming races and today's
star runners and track-and-field athletes

Official Web Site of the Olympic Movement: Athletics
www.olympic.org/uk/sports/programme/index_uk.asp?SportCode=AT
For information on events and the history of track-and-field

USA Track and Field
www.usatf.org
Read athletes' biographies and learn more about sports records

INDEX

batons, 11
Bekele, Kenenisa, 21

Cheeseborough, Chandra, 23
circumference, 9, 10
clothing, 14, 26
competitions, 4, 5, 6–7, 8, 20
competitors, 4
courses, 8
cross-country running, 8

El Guerrouj, Hicham, 18–19
endurance, 4, 14, 28
equipment, 13, 14, 15, 26, 27
exchange zone, 11
exercise, 25, 27

fell running, 8
fouls, 15

Gatlin, Justin, 20
Griffith Joyner, Florence, 22, 23, 24

hurdles, 7, 12

indoor tracks, 9, 10
infield, 6
International Association of Athletics
  Federations (IAAF), 7–8, 13, 21,
  22, 23

Johnson, Michael, 23, 24
jumping events, 6, 7, 12

lanes, 9, 10, 15
legs, 11
long-distance competitions, 11, 13–14

marathons, 8, 28
meets, 6–7, 12
middle-distance competitions, 10–11,
  18–19, 20
mile runs, 10–11, 19
milliseconds, 13, 24
Mutola, Maria, 20

officials, 13, 14, 15
Olympic Games, 5, 7, 12–13,
  16–17, 19, 20, 23–24, 28
Olympic Hall of Fame, 17, 20
outdoor tracks, 9, 10, 26

pain, 28
Parson, Rynell, 22
practice, 22, 28
prize money, 20

records, 13, 17, 19, 21–22, 23–24
relay races, 11–12, 17, 24
road running, 8
Rudolph, Wilma, 16–17, 18, 20
rules, 5, 13, 15

scoring, 12–13
shoes, 15, 26, 27
sidewalks, 27
singlets, 14
socks, 26
spectators, 4, 28
sportsmanship, 27
sprint races, 4, 10, 13, 15, 17,
  21–22, 23, 24
stopwatches, 13, 27
stretching, 28

teams, 11, 12, 14, 24, 25
throwing events, 6–7
track-and-field competitions, 6–7, 12
tracks, 6, 8, 9–10, 11, 25–26
trail running, 8, 27
trails, 27
training, 4, 25

ultramarathons, 8
uniforms, 14
USA Track and Field (USATF), 7

water, 27
water jumps, 7, 8
wind, 13
World Cup competitions, 8

ABOUT THE AUTHORS

Katie Marsico worked as a managing editor in children's publishing before becoming a freelance writer. She lives near Chicago, Illinois, with her husband and two children. She dedicates this book to all the little runners in her family (Sara, Frankie, Emma, Matthew, Maria, Andrew, and, someday soon, C. J. and Addison).

Cecilia Minden, PhD, is a former classroom teacher and university professor. She now enjoys being a full-time author and consultant for children's books. She lives with her family outside Chapel Hill, North Carolina. She dedicates this book to her dog, Kenzie, who believes daily walks should really be daily runs.